SILLY JOKES

Marks and Spencer p.l.c.
Baker Street, London W1U 8EP
www.marksandspencer.com

This edition © Exclusive Editions 2003

This book was created by Magpie Books,
an imprint of Constable & Robinson Ltd

Cover design and inside illustrations courtesy of Mike Phillips

A copy of the British Library Cataloguing-in-Publication
Data is available from the British Library

Printed in China

ISBN 1-84273-966-2

Contents

JOLLY JESTERS

What do you call a spaceship with its
exhaust pipe hanging off?
A space racket.

How do you attract a vegetarian?
Make a noise like a wounded vegetable.

What does a unicorn call its father?
Popcorn.

What do you get if you cross the Devil
with an anagram?
Santa.

What grows between your nose and your chin?
Two lips.

Is it better to write with your right or left hand?
Ideally, you should be writing with a pen, not a hand.

Do moths cry?
Sure. Haven't you ever seen a mothball (bawl)?

Why did the stupid boy wear a turtleneck sweater?
To hide his flea collar.

What happens if you throw a red ruby in the Black Sea?
It gets wet.

What do comets say to each other when they meet?
"Glad to meteor!"

What goes in pink and comes out blue?
A swimmer on a cold day.

What do you get if you cross a chemical with a bicycle?
Bike carbonate of soda.

What are you if you step into a
cow pat?
An incowpoop.

Why did Julius Caesar buy crayons?
He wanted to Mark Antony.

What's sweet and cold and hurtles up
the M1 on a stick?
An articulated lolly.

What goes "Oooooo"?
A cow with no lips.

Where do astronauts keep their sandwiches?
In a launch box.

Why did the farmer plough his field
with a steamroller?
He wanted to grow mashed potatoes.

What did the big weevil say to the
little weevil?
"You're the lesser of two weevils."

Can you spell eighty in two letters?
A T.

How do you know you are being haunted
by a parrot?
*It keeps saying "Ooo's a pretty boy
then?"*

Why is a mouse like hay?
Because the cat'll (cattle) eat it.

What shoes do you make from
banana skins?
Slippers.

What do you get if you cross a cricket
ball and an alien?
A bowling green.

What's the difference between a
policeman and a soldier?
*You'll get arrested if you try dipping a
policeman in your egg.*

Why is a shirt with eight buttons so interesting?
Because you fascinate (fasten eight).

Why did the coffee taste like mud?
Because it was ground that morning.

What do you do if you split your sides laughing?
Run till you get a stitch.

How can you make seven even?
Take away the letter S.

Why does a lion kneel before it springs?
Because it is preying.

What kind of driver doesn't need a licence?
A screwdriver.

Did you hear about the man who crossed the Alps twice without taking a bath?
The dirty double-crosser!

Where did the pilgrims land when they went to America?
On their feet.

How is it that the oldest man in the world doesn't have a grey hair on his head?
He's completely bald.

What did the football fan get when he listened to the match?
A burnt ear.

What is a sleeping bag?
A knapsack.

What do you get if you cross a pudding with a cow pat?
A smelly jelly.

What happened to the man who drank a
bottle of lavatory cleaner?
He went clean round the bend.

What swings through the jungle on
vines backwards?
Nazrat.

What bus has crossed the Atlantic?
Columbus.

How do you file a nail?
Under the letter N.

Did you hear about the peanuts that
walked down a dark alley?
One was assaulted.

What's the difference between a deadly disease and a Klingon?
One's smallpox and the other mauls Spock.

What spacious car lives in a French cathedral?
The Hatchback of Notre Dame.

Why do rabbits eat rust?
Because it's a type of car rot.

What do you get if you cross a pig with a naked person?
Streaky bacon.

19

What gets smaller the more you put in it?
A hole.

How does Luke Skywalker get from planet to planet?
Ewoks.

What do you call a policeman with blonde hair?
A fair cop.

What do you call a pen with no hair?
A bald point.

Why is Saturday night important to
Julius' girlfriend?
Because that's when Julius Caesar.

Why was the Scout so dizzy?
He spent all day doing good turns.

What do you call a man with photos of
Cardiff, Swansea and Bangor?
The Prints of Wales.

Why are oranges like bells?
They peel.

What does a dentist call his X-rays?
Tooth pics.

What colour is a hiccup?
Burple.

What happened to the man who couldn't tell the difference between soap and putty?
His armpits stuck together and all his windows fell out.

How do you make a lemon drop?
Let go of it.

What's a dimple?
An upside-down pimple.

23

Did you hear about the cross-eyed teacher?
He couldn't control his pupils.

Why do bakers work late?
They knead the dough.

What makes a good librarian?
Shelf control.

What do you get if you cross a cow with a grass cutter?
A lawn mooer.

Which great Arab invented crisps?
Sultan Vinegar.

Why was the musician arrested?
He was always getting into treble.

What do you get hanging from trees in
the jungle?
Sore arms.

How does a broom act?
With sweeping gestures.

What's worse than finding a maggot in your apple?
Finding half a maggot in your apple.

Why should you take a few big bags of rubbish to restaurants?
It's polite to leave a tip.

What's the most important thing to remember in a Chemistry lesson?
Never lick the spoon.

What did the ice cream say to the unhappy cake?
"Hey, what's eating you?"

What's purple and hums?
An electric plum.

What did the big chimney say to the little chimney?
"You're too young to smoke!"

Why do the French never eat two eggs for breakfast?
Because one egg is un oeuf.

What kind of nut do you hang pictures on?
A walnut.

What did one keyboard say to the other keyboard?
Sorry, you're not my type.

What does an educated owl say?
"Who-o-o-m."

Why are orchestras so badly behaved?
They don't know how to conduct themselves.

What do you get if you cross a shoulder bag with a mallard?
A ducksack.

What's the difference between roast
beef and pea soup?
Anyone can roast beef.

What did the mouse say to the camera?
Cheese.

Where do snowmen put their
web pages?
On the winternet.

How can you double your money?
Look at it in a mirror.

What do you call a Victorian ant?
An antique.

Did you hear about the man who tried to cross the Atlantic on a plank of wood?
He couldn't find a plank long enough.

What's green and rocks?
Elvis Parsley.

Why did the lamp-post blush?
It saw the traffic light changing.

What do you call a group of cars?
A clutch.

Why are brides so unlucky?
They never marry the best man.

What should you do if your dog chases anyone on a bicycle?
Take away his bicycle.

What do you get if you cross a computer with a hamburger?
A big mac.

What do you get if you cross a football team with a bunch of crazy jokers?
Mad-jester United.

Where's the best place to dance in California?
San Frandisco.

What's brown and sticky?
A stick.

How do chickens start a race?
From scratch.

What did the electric plug say to the wall?
"Socket to me."

Why shouldn't you swim on a full stomach?
It's much easier swimming in a full swimming pool.

What did the plumber say to his girlfriend?
"It's all over, Flo!"

What tool do you use in maths lessons?
Multi-pliers.

Where does a snowman put his birthday candles?
On his birthday flake.

Why did the spaceship land outside the girl's bedroom?
She must have left the landing light on.

What's the largest table in school?
The multiplication table.

Which pets make the most noise?
Trumpets.

What do football managers do when the pitch becomes waterlogged?
Bring on the subs.

What do you call a greasy chicken?
A slick chick.

What did the boy do when he was
offered rock cakes for tea?
He took his pick.

Did you hear that thieves have broken
into a dogs' home?
Police are following a number of leads.

What do you call a cheese that
isn't yours?
Nacho cheese.

What do you get if you cross a footballer
with a mythical creature?
A centaur forward.

How many balls of string would it take
to reach the moon?
Just one really long one would do it.

What colour is a cheerleader?
Yeller.

Who drives all his customers away but
still makes a living?
A taxi driver.

What did the bee say to the rose?
"Hi, Bud."

What's a forum?
A two-um plus a two-um.

Why did the man clamber up the roof
of the pub?
The drinks were on the house.

Why does the ocean roar?
*You would too if you had crabs on
your bottom!*

What do you get if you cross a pig with
a part in a film?
A ham role.

What's sweet and sour and very violent?
Kung food.

What do you call a vicar on a motorbike?
Rev.

What do you call a spaceship that drips water?
A crying saucer.

What do you call an igloo without a toilet?
An ig.

What do ants use for hula hoops?
Cheerios.

What do you use baby oil for?
Squeaky infants.

Why is Sunday stronger than Monday?
Because Monday is a weak day.

What fly has laryngitis?
A hoarsefly.

What did the bow tie say to the boy?
You double-crossed me.

What happened to the sardine when it
was late for work?
It was canned.

Why did the grandmother put wheels on
her rocking chair?
She liked to rock and roll.

Why do tape machines always win
football matches?
They have fast forwards.

What do you get if you cross a sports
reporter with a vegetable?
A common 'tater.

How does a really small person say goodbye?
He microwaves.

What do you call a pistachio in space?
An astronut.

Can you spell a composition with two letters?
S A (essay).

What do you get if you cross a hairdresser with a bucket of cement?
Permanent waves.

When is a car not a car?
When it turns into a garage.

What's the difference between a train
and a tree?
*One leaves its shed and the other
sheds its leaves.*

What do you call a fairy that
doesn't wash?
Stinkerbell.

What do you get if you cross a
toadstool with a suitcase?
Not mushroom for your holiday clothes.

How many peas are there in a pint?
There's only one P in pint.

Spell a Native American tent with two letters.
T P.

What do you call an amusing horse racer?
A jokey.

What food is good for the brain?
Noodle soup.

Why can you never get hungry in the desert?
Because of all the sand which is there.

47

What did the pen say to the paper?
I dot an "i" on you.

What newspaper do cows read?
The Daily Moos.

Where is Felixstowe?
On the end of Felix's foot.

What do you call a hearing aid made from fruit?
A lemonade.

What part of a car is the laziest?
The wheels. They're always tired.

What is everyone's favourite tree?
A poplar tree.

Why did the football manager give his team lighters?
Because they kept losing their matches.

How does Moby Dick celebrate his birthday?
He has a whale of a time.

How many ears does Captain Kirk have?
A left ear, a right ear and a final frontier.

What tricks do eggs play on each other?
Practical yolks.

What does dirty rain do?
It showers.

What goes around everywhere?
Belts.

Why was the little chimney ill?
It caught flu.

What do you call a boy whose father is an AK47?
A son of a gun.

Why is a lazy boy nothing like Robinson Crusoe?
Robinson Crusoe got all his work done by Friday.

What do you get if you cross an alligator with King Midas?
A croc of gold.

What is the best time of year to dig up carrots?
When the farmer is on holiday.

What has four eyes and runs for over two thousand miles?
The Mississippi River.

What do you call a woman with egg, beans and chips on her head?
Caff.

What has fifty heads and fifty tails?
Fifty pennies.

What Roman numeral can climb a wall?
IV.

What did one eye say to the other?
"Between us something smells."

What's the difference between someone who's desperate for the lavatory and someone who's trapped in the lions' enclosure?
One is dying to go and the other is going to die.

Why won't prawns share their toys?
They're shellfish.

How does a leopard change its spots?
Easy, it gets up from one spot and walks over to a new one.

What's orange and sounds like a parrot?
A carrot.

What do you get if you cross a chicken with an electricity socket?
A battery hen.

What kind of dog loves to take bubble
baths?
A shampoodle.

What do naughty cats leave behind
after a picnic?
Kitty litter.

What do toads sit on?
Toadstools.

Which insect makes films?
Steven Spielbug.

What goes, "Clippety–clippety–clippety"?
A three-legged horse galloping.

What do you get if you cross a cow, a sheep and a baby goat?
The milky baa kid.

Why was the monkey taken in for questioning?
They wanted to gorilla.

What do you get if you cross a pig with a laundry?
Hogwash.

What goes, "Dot-dot-dot-croak, dash-dot-dash-croak..."?
Morse toad.

Why are chickens so disgusting?
Because they're fowl.

If an animal with four legs is a quadruped and an animal with two legs is a biped, what's a zebra?
Stri-ped.

What do you get if you cross a dog with a film studio?
Collie-wood.

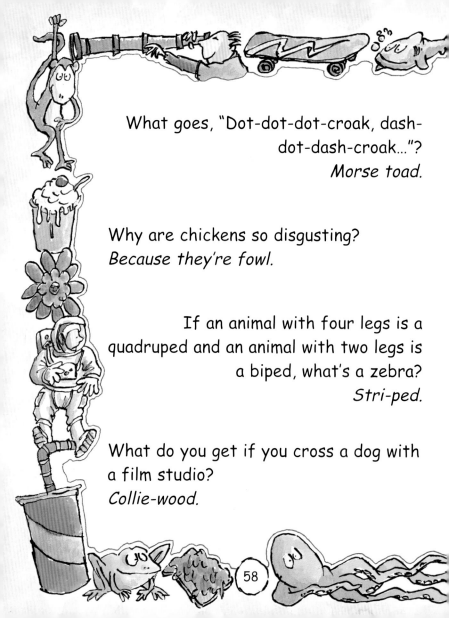

Why was the cow shivering?
It was Friesian.

How do you stop a cobra from striking?
Pay it decent wages.

What did the parrot say to the spaniel?
"I'm a cocker too."

What did the Pink Panther say when he stepped on an ant?
(sing) "Dead ant, dead ant, dead ant, dead ant, dead ant, dead ant, dead ant..."

What do you get if you cross a mouse with a bottle of olive oil?
A squeak that oils itself.

Where do good turkeys go when
they die?
To oven.

What's cool and always out of breath?
The Pink Panter.

What do you call a chicken that eats
cement?
A bricklayer.

What insect can be spelled with just
one letter?
Bee.

What do you call a horse sunbathing behind some iron railings?
A zebra.

Why didn't the viper vipe 'er nose?
Because the adder 'ad 'er hanky.

How do Spanish musicians catch fish?
They castanet.

What do you call a parrot when it has dried itself after a bath?
Polly unsaturated.

Why did the fly fly?
Because the spider spied 'er.

What's the difference between a school
dinner and a pile of slugs?
A school dinner has a plate.

Why are adolescent geese so shy?
They get goose pimples.

What do you get if you divide the
circumference of a pig by its diameter?
Pork pi.

What do you call a bee that is always complaining?
A grumble bee.

Why are pigs such good letter writers?
They have loads of pen pals.

Why do bees have sticky hair?
Because they have honeycombs.

What is a bee with a low buzz?
A mumble bee.

What do you call a juvenile octopus delinquent?
A crazy, mixed-up squid.

How do you stop moles digging up your garden?
Hide their spades.

What do two lovesick owls say when it's raining?
"Too-wet-to-woo!"

What do you get if you cross a snake with a building site?
A boa constructor.

What fish do you keep in a birdcage?
A perch.

Why did the zookeeper split the gnus up?
Because he had good gnus and bad gnus.

Why did the gorilla log on to the Internet?
To send chimpanzee-mail.

What do hedgehogs have for lunch?
Prickled onions.

What is a parrot?
A wordy birdy.

Why is it a bad idea to gamble in the jungle?
There are too many cheetahs about.

What kind of snake is turned on when it's raining?
The windscreen viper.

What's the difference between a fly and a bird?
A bird can fly but a fly can't bird.

What do you get if you cross a parrot with an alarm clock?
Politics.

Why did the woodpecker with no beak
listen to heavy metal?
It was a headbanger.

What has more lives than a cat?
A frog — it croaks every night.

What should you do with a wombat?
Play wom.

What films do vultures love?
Carrion films.

How do you keep flies out of the kitchen?
Coat the dining room in manure.

What do you call a film about mallards?
A duckumentary.

What has four legs, no sense of humour and flies?
A dead hyena.

What do you get if you cross a mountain with a baby?
A cry for Alp.

What do you call a pig that studies karate?
A pork chop.

What do you get if you cross a horse with a skunk?
Whinny the Pooh.

What's the difference between a wolf and a flea?
One howls on the prairie and the other prowls on the hairy.

What's a dog's favourite city?
New York-ie.

What do you call a rabbit dressed up as a cake?
A cream bunny.

What's brown and has a trunk?
A mouse returning from holiday.

What did the slug say to the snail?
"Hey, nice crash helmet!"

Why did the two lovesick deer run away?
They wanted to antelope.

What's cute, brown and sticky, and eats eucalyptus leaves?
Coca-koala.

Why did the chicken cross the web?
To get to the other site.

Where do birds meet for coffee?
In a nest café.

Why was the sheep so itchy?
It was covered in fleece.

When do mice follow cats?
In a dictionary.

Where's Spiderman's home page?
On the World Wide Web.

Why couldn't the cow give milk?
It was an udder failure.

Did you hear about the skunk that was
shot into space?
It stank to high heaven.

Why was the fly-fisherman so happy?
He caught a four-pound bluebottle.

What do you call a blind dinosaur?
I-don't-think-he-saurus.

What do you call an ant with five pairs of eyes?
Ant-ten-eye.

How many ants does it take to fill a flat?
Ten ants.

What's the best way to get a wild hippo?
Find a tame one and call it names.

Why did the lunatic catch so many squirrels?
He kept climbing trees and acting like a nut.

What kind of dog gets everything wrong?
A cock-up spaniel.

What's smaller than a gnat's mouth?
A gnat's dinner.

What do you get if you cross a cow with an out-of-date map?
Udderly lost.

How do lions recharge their laptops?
They plug them into the manes.

What do you get if you cross a frog and
a rabbit?
Ribbit!

What did the lobster say to the rock
pool?
"Show me your mussels!"

Why was the butterfly turned away
from the dance?
Because it was a moth ball.

What do you get if you cross a bee with
a coach?
A buzzzz.

79

What lives in Tibet and spends too long on the phone?
A yak.

What do you call a snake without any clothes on?
Snaked.

What do cats eat for dessert?
Mice pudding.

How does a flea get from place to place?
By itch-hiking.

Why are snails' shells so shiny?
They use snail varnish.

What kind of tiles shouldn't you use for
your bathroom walls?
Reptiles.

What do you get if you cross a bear
with a freezer?
A teddy brrr.

Why did the bees go on strike?
*For more honey and shorter working
flowers.*

Why don't you see millipedes playing football?
By the time they've laced up their boots, the final whistle's blown.

What goes oink, baaa, moo, quack, woof, meow?
A multilingual pig.

What book tells you about chickens?
A hencyclopaedia.

What do you get if you cross a skeleton with a dog?
An animal that buries itself.

What's grey and squirts you with jam?
A mouse eating a doughnut.

Did all the animals in Noah's Ark come in pairs?
No, the worms came in apples.

How do you find a princess?
You follow the foot prince.

What do farmers use to dig up their potato crop?
A spud hound.

What do you get if you cross a monster with a chicken?
Free-strange eggs.

What's the difference between a buffalo and a bison?
You can't wash your hands in a buffalo.

What do fleas do if it's too late to walk to school?
Take the dog.

Why does a heron stand on one leg?
It would fall over if it lifted both.

How can you tell if a bee is on the phone?
You get a buzzy signal.

What's pink and hard?
A flamingo with a bazooka.

What did the bee say to its
naughty child?
"Please beehive!"

How many skunks does it take to make a
really big stink?
A phew!

What do you get if you cross a compass
with a shellfish?
A guided mussel.

86

Why are owls cleverer than chickens?
Have you ever eaten Kentucky Fried Owl?

Why did the lettuce die?
It got a slug in its heart.

Where do hamsters come from?
Hamsterdam.

Why did the lobster blush?
Because the sea weed.

Why did the crab get arrested?
Because he was always pinching things.

How did the glow worm feel when
someone stepped on his tail?
De-lighted.

What happens if you give your mouse
some smelly cheese?
*You make an awful mess of your
computer.*

How do little rattlesnakes call home?
Poison-to-poison.

Why do birds fly south in winter?
It's too far to walk.

What do you get if you cross a toad
with a galaxy?
Star warts.

What lies on the ground a thousand
feet up and smells?
A dead millipede.

What is the opposite of restaurant?
Workerant.

What do you call a camel with three humps?
Humphrey.

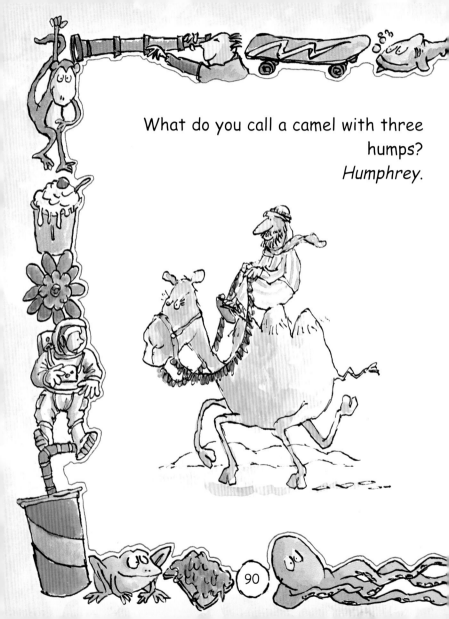

Where do ants buy their cheese
and wine?
Frants.

Why did the man drag a cabbage
on a lead?
He thought it was a collie.

Where do crows get their beer?
A crowbar.

What do you get if you cross a cow with
a jogging machine?
A milk shake.

What did the bookworm say to the librarian?
"Can I burrow this book, please?"

How do you catch an elephant fish?
Use peanuts for bait.

Why did the hedgehog cross the road?
He wanted to fetch his squash partner.

What do you get if you cross a sheep with a spaceship?
Apollo neck jumper.

What do you call a rabbit that has its
own private jet?
A millionhare.

What did the banana do when the
monkey chased it?
The banana split.

What do small cats drink?
Condensed milk.

What do you get if you cross a
Shakespeare play with a pig?
A Ham omelette.

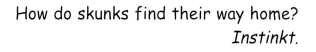

How do skunks find their way home?
Instinkt.

How can you get across the African
plains at 60 mph?
Strap yourself to a cheetah.

What's black and white and never
grows up?
Peter Pan-da.

What do you get if you cross a penguin
with an elk?
Chocolate moose.

What did the sow say to the pig?
"You take me for grunted."

What happened to the prawn that went to a disco?
It pulled a mussel.

What has a coat in winter and pants in the sun?
A dog.

Why is this newt I bought so small?
Because it's my newt.

What do you get if you cross a kangaroo with a skyscraper?
A high jumper.

What did the buffalo say to his son
when he left the house?
"Bison."

Where do horses spend their
honeymoons?
The bridle suite.

What do you call an insect that can't
remember the words?
A humbug.

What kind of animal tells little
white lies?
An amphibian.

Why did the donkey have so few friends?
It always made an ass of itself.

What do you call a cat that has just eaten a whole duck?
A duck-filled fatty-puss.

How do sheep heat their houses?
Central bleating.

What sleeps at the bottom of the sea?
A kipper.

What's purple, 10,000 km long and can
be seen from space?
The grape wall of China.

What do you get if you cross an ape
with twelve egg whites and a bag of
sugar?
A meringue-utan.

Why did the butterfly?
Because it saw the milk float.

What is the science of shopping?
Biology.

What did the horse say when it was put in a field full of thistles?
"Thistle have to do!"

What do you get if you put ducks in a blender?
Cream quackers.

Where do cats that lose their tails go?
A retailer.

What do pigs and old telephones have in common?
All that crackling.

How do frogs die?
They Kermit suicide.

What do horses play in their spare time?
Stable tennis.

What do skunks play in their spare time?
Ping pong.

What kind of meat doesn't stand up?
Lean meat.

HAPPY
HOWLERS

What language do they speak in Cuba?
Cubic.

Why couldn't the wigwam and tepee get to sleep?
Because they were two tents.

What instrument did they play in the Middle Ages?
The Anglo-saxophone.

What do you get if you cross a skeleton, a feather and a joke book?
Rib ticklers.

What's the best way to make a coat last?
Make the trousers first.

Why did the seaweed blush?
Because it saw the ship's bottom.

What is a bunsen burner used for?
Burning bunsens.

What do you get if you cross a skeleton with a tumble drier?
Bone-dry clothes.

When is a grown man still a child?
When he's a miner.

What do you get if you wash your greenhouse?
Broken glass in the washing machine.

How do you strain vegetables?
Make them do a hundred press-ups and a ten-mile run.

How do you get a baby astronaut to sleep?
Rock it.

What should you never forget to take
into the Sahara Desert?
A thirst-aid kit.

What's the difference between a cat
and a comma?
*One has claws at the end of her paws
and the other has a pause at the end of
a clause.*

What's a spaceman's favourite meal?
Launch.

What kind of paper can you tear?
Terrible paper.

Why was the man with £1999.99 in his hands unwell?
He wasn't feeling too grand.

What did the hungry alien say when he landed on Earth?
"Take me to your larder!"

What do computer experts do at weekends?
Go for a disk drive.

How do you make hot cross buns?
Lock buns in a room and turn the heating up high.

What do people do in clock factories?
They make faces all day.

What's purple and screams?
A damson in distress.

Can April March?
No, but August May.

How do you make a Swiss roll?
Push him off a mountain.

What do a footballer and a magician
have in common?
Both do hat tricks.

What's got four legs, a trunk and lots of keys?
A piano up a tree.

What did Santa say to his wife on Christmas Eve?
"Don't go out in the reindeer."

What do you get if you cross the Amazonian rainforest with a map of Norwich?
Very lost.

What kind of water can't freeze?
Hot water.

Why did the hotel manager ask the talkative chess players to leave his hotel?
He didn't like chess nuts boasting in an open foyer.

Why did the tomato go out with the mushroom?
Because he was a fungi.

How was the Roman Empire cut in half?
With a pair of Caesars.

What do you get if you stuff your computer's disk drive with herbs?
A thyme machine.

Where are the Andes?
On the end of the armies.

What's the difference between a
photocopier and the measles?
*One makes facsimiles and the other
makes sick families.*

What is ET short for?
So he can touch his toes.

Where is the best place to buy
computer software?
Washington CD.

What has four wheels and goes, "Hic! Hic! Hic!"?
A hiccup truck.

What's full of holes but can still hold water?
A sponge.

What did the boy say to get his big brother to give back his building bricks?
"Lego!"

What pet is always found on the floor?
A carpet.

Why was the man with a photographic memory so unhappy?
He kept having negative thoughts.

What did the man with two left feet
wear to the beach?
Flip-flips.

Did you hear about the boy who was
named after his father?
He was called "Dad".

What position in the football team were
the railings?
In defence.

When is a chair like a fabric?
When it's sat in.

What crisps can fly?
Plain crisps.

What's white and yellow and goes at 125 mph?
A train driver's egg sandwich.

What should you do if you need directions in space?
Askeroid.

What do you call a man with two left feet?
Whatever you like. If he tries to catch you, he'll just run round in circles.

What do you do if your nose goes
on strike?
Picket.

What's brown, hairy and sneezes?
A coconut with a cold.

What's the difference between a cross-
word expert, a greedy boy and glue?
*One's a good puzzler and the other's a
pud guzzler. The glue is where you
get stuck.*

Where was Solomon's temple?
On his head.

What do you call coconut trees that exercise a lot?
Sweaty palms.

What do snowmen do in cold weather?
Sit round a candle.

What do snowmen do in very cold weather?
Light it.

Why did the computer act crazy?
It had a screw loose.

Why did the boy blush when he opened the fridge?
He saw the salad dressing.

Where would you find a rubber trombone?
In an elastic band.

Did you hear about the butcher who sat on his mincing machine?
He got a little behind in his orders.

What happened when the plastic surgeon went to sleep in front of the fire?
He melted.

Which end of a bus is it best to get off?
It doesn't matter. Both ends stop.

What did the princess say while she was waiting for her photos to arrive?
"Some day my prints will come!"

Why was the man so happy that his career was in ruins?
He was an archaeologist.

What travels around the world but stays in a corner?
A stamp.

Why did the cowboy ride his horse?
Because the horse was too heavy to carry.

How do footballers keep cool?
They stand next to the fans.

What stays hot in the fridge?
Chilli sauce.

Who sits on Cinderella's keyboard?
Buttons.

What do you call an overweight ET?
An extra cholesterol.

Why do oranges wear sun block?
Because they peel.

What do you get if you cross a vampire
with a circus entertainer?
*Something that goes straight for the
juggler.*

How do you know when a clock is
hungry?
It goes back four seconds.

What do you get if you cross a jogger
with an apple pie?
Puff pastry.

When did nerds rule the Earth?
The Dork Ages.

Why did the sword swallower go to prison?
He coughed and killed two people.

Why did the golfer wear two pairs of trousers?
In case he got a hole in one.

What do you call a dentist in the army?
A drill sergeant.

Why are rivers so wealthy?
They are lined with banks.

Why did the robot need a manicure?
It had rusty nails.

What illness do overloaded Christmas trees get?
Tinselitis.

Why did the man put a clock under his desk?
He wanted to work overtime.

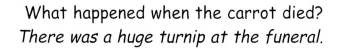

What happened when the carrot died?
There was a huge turnip at the funeral.

What happens if you play table tennis
with a rotten egg?
First it goes ping, then it goes pong.

How does the moon cut the sun's hair?
Eclipse it.

What has fifty feet but can't walk?
A tape measure.

What do you call someone who makes
half-size models of fish?
A scale modeller.

When do computers go to sleep?
When it's internight.

Where do the police put trifle thieves?
In custardy.

What did the biscuit say when he saw
his brother being run over?
"Crumbs!"

What do you call someone who draws
funny pictures of motor vehicles?
A car-toonist.

Where was the Magna Carta signed?
At the bottom.

Why did the girl name her cat
"Blacksmith"?
*Whenever she called it, it made a bolt
for the door.*

What do you get if you cross a waiter
and a slippery floor?
Flying saucers.

Why shouldn't you believe a person
in bed?
Because he is lying.

129

What do you get if you cross a pen with
Napoleon's feet?
A footnote in history.

What's short, green and goes camping?
A boy sprout.

What is a volcano?
A mountain with indigestion.

How do bank robbers send messages?
By flee mail.

What can fall thousands of feet onto iron railings and not get hurt?
A plane's shadow.

What is the hardest subject?
The study of rocks.

How do you find white shirts on the Internet?
Use a starch engine.

What do you call a musical instrument that is played by two teams of twenty people?
A piano forte.

Why couldn't the parsnip buy a drink in
the pub one afternoon?
They didn't serve food after two o'clock.

Why can't cars play football?
They've only got one boot.

What's the difference between bogies
and broccoli?
Children don't eat broccoli.

What do you call the owner of a tool
factory?
The vice chairman.

Did you hear about the man who fell
into a vat of curry?
He slipped into a korma.

What happened when two televisions got married?
It was an awful wedding, but the reception was great.

Who invented King Arthur's round table?
Sir Circumference.

What colour is the wind?
Blew.

What do you say when an aeroplane disappears over the horizon?
Boeing, going, gone.

Where were the kings of Albania
crowned?
On the head.

Why was Cleopatra so difficult to get
on with?
She was the Queen of Denial.

For pigs, what came after the
Stone Age and the Bronze Age?
The sausage.

Why was the girl named Sugar?
Because she was so refined.

Why did the tap dancer leave his job?
He kept falling in the sink.

What did the orange squash say to the water?
"I'm diluted to see you!"

Which two words in the English language have the most letters?
Post office.

What tables don't you have to learn?
Dinner tables.

Who is the oldest singer on the
Internet?
Click Jagger.

What has four wheels and flies?
A rubbish truck.

Why are two thieves like underwear?
Because they're a pair of nickers.

What is the cheapest time to call your
friends long distance?
When they're not home.

What are deck chairs made of?
Beach trees.

How can you prevent diseases caused by biting insects?
Don't bite any insects.

What happened to the girl who wanted a puppy for Christmas?
She had to have turkey like everyone else.

Why was the headmaster worried?
There were too many rulers in school.

What does Luke Skywalker shave with?
A laser blade.

What's brown and steaming and comes out of Cowes?
The Isle of Wight ferry.

Which two letters are bad for your teeth?
D K.

When does a telephone work underwater?
When it's wringing wet.

Where does Tarzan buy his clothes?
A jungle sale.

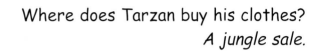

A greengrocer is six feet tall, has a forty inch waist and size eleven shoes. What does he weigh?
Vegetables.

What kind of food do you get at a nuclear power station?
Fission chips.

What do you put in a www.ashing machine?
Net curtains.

Why did the teacher put the lights on?
The class was so dim.

What do you call a man who is half man, half king of the jungle?
Richard the Lionhalf.

What is bought by the yard and worn by the foot?
A carpet.

Why did the woman rub grease all over her face before she went to bed?
She needed to get up oily the next morning.

Where do astronauts leave their spaceships?
At parking meteors.

Where would you find secret soup?
The minestrone of defence.

If a white house is made of white bricks, and a red house of red bricks, what's a greenhouse made of?
Glass.

How do you stop your laptop's batteries from running out?
Hide its trainers.

What do you get when you cross a telephone with a pair of trousers?
Bell-bottoms.

What do you call a woman who can balance ten pints of beer on her head?
Beatrix.

What do you call a woman with ten pints of beer on her head playing snooker?
Beatrix Potter.

Why don't astronauts have parties in space?
There's no atmosphere.

What is ice?
Skid stuff.

Why did the chilly fishermen sink when they lit a fire in their kayak?
Because you can't have your kayak and heat it.

What has sixty feet and sings out of tune?
The school choir.

What begins with T, ends with T and is filled with tea?
A teapot.

What do you get if you cross a bike with a rose?
Bicycle petals.

How did the madman go through the forest?
Along the psycho path.

Why do ducks watch the news?
To get the feather forecast.

What's a doughnut?
A person who is crazy about money.

Why did the Romans build straight roads?
So their soldiers wouldn't go around the bend.

Why are pianos hard to open?
The keys are inside.

Did you hear about the man who
drowned in a bowl of muesli?
A strong currant pulled him under.

Who succeeded the first President of
the USA?
The second one.

Why was the computer in pain?
It had a slipped disk.

GIGANTIC GAGS

What's the biggest mouse in the world?
A hippopotamouse.

What weighs three tons and wears glass slippers?
Cinderellaphant.

How did the giant destroy three countries when he was on holiday?
He picked up Turkey, dunked it in Greece and fried it in Japan.

Why was the computer so thin?
Because it hadn't had many bytes.

What are the biggest ants in the world?
Giants.

What are the second biggest ants in the world?
Elephants.

How do you attract King Kong?
Hang upside down in a tree and make a noise like a banana.

What do you get if you cross a very bent piece of wood with a spaceship?
Warp factor nine.

When can three giant dinosaurs get
under an umbrella and not get wet?
When it isn't raining.

What starts with E, ends with E and
only has one letter?
An envelope.

What do you get if dinosaurs have a
car crash?
Tyrannosaurus wrecks.

What holds the moon up?
Moon beams.

What's big and grey and has trouble with personal hygiene?
A smellephant.

What should you do if you go on a picnic with King Kong?
Give him the biggest bananas.

Why do elephants have trunks?
They'd never fit all their clothes in a suitcase.

Why do squirrels like to sit on telephone poles?
To stay away from the nuts on the ground.

What do you get if you cross a pig with a dinosaur?
Jurassic pork.

Where would you find a rhinoceros with no legs?
Wherever you left it.

What do you give elephants with big feet?
Big shoes.

What do you get if you cross a cow with a crystal ball?
A message from the udder side.

What weighs two tons and sticks to the roof of your mouth?
Peanut butter and rhino sandwiches.

What do you get if you hunt bear?
Locked up for indecent exposure.

What do you give an elephant to help it sleep?
Trunkquillizers.

What did the birthday balloon say to the pin?
"Hi, Buster."

What did the pitcher say to the cup?
I'll have none of your lip.

What did the window say to the Venetian blind?
If it weren't for you, it would be curtains for me.

What do you call a man who forgets to put his underpants on?
Nicholas.

Why did the hippo put on a yellow wig?
To see if blondes have more fun.

What do you get if you cross a telephone with a ghost?
A phantom caller.

What do you get if you cross a rhino with a spider?
A rhino that has trouble getting out of your bath.

How do dinosaurs pass exams?
With extinction.

Why don't elephants use computers?
They're afraid of the mouse.

Why couldn't prehistoric man send birthday cards?
The stamps kept falling off the rocks.

What does a triceratops sit on?
Its tricera-bottom.

What happened to the man who dreamt
he was eating a giant marshmallow?
*He woke up coughing feathers and
found that his pillow was missing.*

What did Delaware?
She wore her New Jersey.

What's the best way to find out an
elephant's age?
Check his driver's licence.

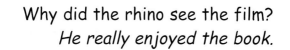

Why did the rhino see the film?
He really enjoyed the book.

How do you get a hippo to the top of an oak tree?
Strap it to an acorn and wait fifty years.

What do you get if you cross King Kong with a flock of pigeons?
Trafalgar Square knee deep in dung.

Why did the fat monster put a candle on his tummy?
He was celebrating his girthday.

What do you call a gorilla with bananas
in its ears?
Anything you like, it can't hear you.

What happened to the elephant that
had too much whisky?
It got trunk.

What's big, strong, green and very
tough to chew?
The Inedible Hulk.

What is an elf's favourite kind of
birthday cake?
Shortcake.

Have you heard the one about the giant fruit cake?
It's very hard to swallow.

What did the boy banana say to the girl banana?
You have a lot of appeal.

What do grizzlies take with them on holiday?
Just the bear essentials.

What do you get if you cross a crocodile with a camera?
A snapshot.

161

Why are giraffes so cheap to feed?
A little goes a long way.

What's the best time of year to see a man-eating tiger?
I don't know — but at Christmas, it's easy to see a man eating turkey.

What do elephants wear under their trousers?
Elepants.

Why are elephants tall, grey and wrinkly?
Because if they were small, white and smooth, they would be aspirins.

What do you get if you cross a telephone with a dog?
A golden receiver.

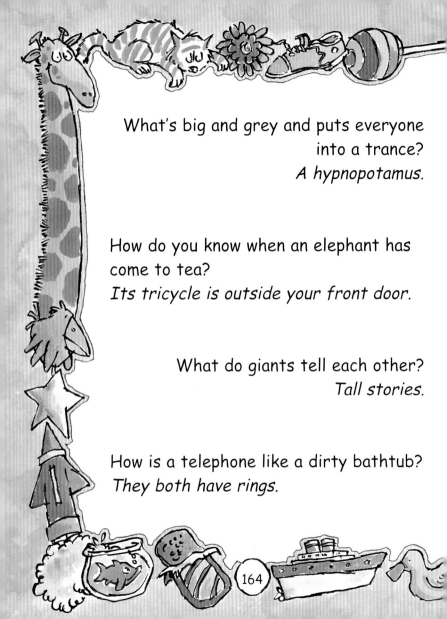

What's big and grey and puts everyone
into a trance?
A hypnopotamus.

How do you know when an elephant has
come to tea?
Its tricycle is outside your front door.

What do giants tell each other?
Tall stories.

How is a telephone like a dirty bathtub?
They both have rings.

What did the boy gopher say to the girl gopher?
I gopher you.

What do you call a woman with a sheep on her head?
Baa-baa-ra.

How many people can fit into the world's largest stadium when it's empty?
One — after that, it's no longer empty.

Why couldn't the skunk use her phone?
It was out of odour.

What's Nelly the Elephant's
middle name?
The.

What's the difference between a hippo
and a banana?
*Try picking it up — if you can't, it's
either a hippo or a giant banana.*

What do whales chew?
Blubber gum.

How does a lobster answer the phone?
"Shello?"

How do you get a rhino out of a phone box?
The same way you got him in.

Why did the elephant leave the circus?
He was fed up with working for peanuts.

What should you do if a rhino charges?
Pay it and run.

How can you tell if someone with curly hair is on the phone?
You get a frizzy signal.

What is another name for a telephone booth?
A chatterbox.

When do tigers eat people?
Chewsdays.

What grows on the World Wide Web and stings?
Internettles.

How can you tell if someone who's having a temper tantrum is on the phone?
You get a tizzy signal.

Why did the hen cross the road?
To prove he wasn't chicken.

What did the jack say to the car?
"Can I give you a lift?"

Why did the hippo wear red braces?
To hold up his red trousers.

Where do you find giant snails?
On the end of giants' fingers.

When does a horse talk on the phone?
Whinny wants to.

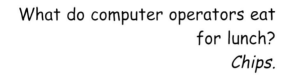

What do computer operators eat
for lunch?
Chips.

How powerful is the squirt from an
elephant's trunk?
*Very — a jumbo jet can keep five
hundred people in the air for hours on
end.*

What's the biggest prehistoric insect?
The mam-moth.

What do you get if you cross a phone
with a pair of glasses?
A television.

Why did the giant have a pocket calculator?
To work out how many pockets he had.

Why did the big game hunter stop hunting elephants?
He got tired of carrying around the decoys.

What's king of the jungle and wears a boater and a stripy blazer?
A dandy lion.

What did the big ape say when he dialled incorrectly?
"Oops. King Kong ring wrong."

Why is King Kong big and hairy?
*So you can distinguish him from a
gooseberry.*

What fruit does a gorilla sleep on?
An ape-ri-cot.

What do you call sleeping prehistoric
monsters?
Dinosnores.

How does a baboon make phone calls?
He just monkeys around on the line.

What's the difference between an elephant and a bad pen?
One rarely bites and the other barely writes.

Why did King Kong scale the Empire State Building?
The lift was broken.

How can you tell that an elephant has been in your bed?
The sheets smell of peanuts.

How does a barber make phone calls?
He cuts them short.

Why is the Incredible Hulk green?
He's not ripe and needs to be left in the sun for a few days.

What is yellow and grey and has an excellent memory?
An elephant omelette.

Who was the world's strongest thief?
Atlas, because he held up the whole world.

What do you get if you cross a telephone with an iron?
A smooth operator.

What did Hannibal say when he saw the elephants coming?
"Here come the gooseberries!" (He was colour-blind.)

Why does King Kong have two feet?
If he had any more, ants really wouldn't have a chance.

What happened when Nelly the Elephant ran away with the circus?
The police made her bring it back.

What did Fat Stanley win when he lost twelve stone in weight?
The No-belly prize.

What kind of music do phones love to hear?
A symphony.

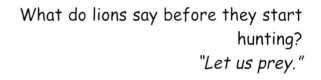

What do lions say before they start
hunting?
"Let us prey."

Why do hippos wallow in mud?
They think it's slick.

What's the difference between African
and Indian elephants?
About three thousand miles.

What do you get if you cross a pig with
a box of itching powder?
Pork scratchings.

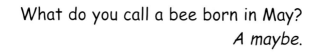

What do you call a bee born in May?
A maybe.

What vegetable is it dangerous to have
aboard ship?
A leek.

What animals were last off the Ark?
*The elephants, because they took a long
time to pack their trunks.*

What has wings, a long tail and
wears a bow?
A birthday pheasant.

Why do gorillas climb trees in the jungle?
There's nothing else to climb in the jungle.

Why is Ireland so rich?
Because its capital is always Dublin.

How do we know that peanuts are fattening?
Have you ever seen a skinny elephant eating peanuts?

What do you get if you cross a cow with a goat?
Butter from a butter.

How hard is it to bury a dead elephant?
Not as hard as trying to bury a living elephant.

Why did cavemen draw pictures of rhinoceroses and hippopotamuses?
It was much easier than spelling their names.

Why is a pencil the heaviest thing in your pocket?
Because it's full of lead.

What's the moral of the story about Jonah and the whale?
You can't keep a good man down.

Why do hippos wear sandals?
Otherwise they would sink into the sand.

What do you call a voodoo elephant?
Mumbo jumbo.

What do lions eat with milk?
Chocolate chimp cookies.

What do you get if you cross an artist with a policeman?
A brush with the law.

What gives money to baby elephants in exchange for teeth?
The tusk fairy.

Why do windows squeak when you
open them?
Because they have panes.

What's purple on the outside and green
on the inside?
*The Incredible Hulk wearing purple
pyjamas.*

Why did the safari guide lose his
driving licence?
He parked on a yellow lion.

What did Noah do to pass the time on
the Ark?
*Fished, but he didn't catch much. He
only had two worms.*

Why doesn't Sweden export cattle?
Because it wants to keep its Stockholm.

What do you get if you cross a
computer with a ballet?
The Netcracker Suite.

How do lions like their steak?
Medium roar.

What happened when the man put his
head into a lion's mouth to count how
many teeth it had?
*The lion closed its mouth to see how
many heads the man had.*

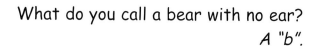

What do you call a bear with no ear?
A "b".

Why do elephants have flat feet?
From jumping off tall trees.

Why couldn't the whales make
themselves understood to the angry
porpoises?
They were speaking at cross porpoises.

What do you get if you cross a TV
programme with a load of sheep?
A flock-u-mentary.

What's the biggest pencil in the world?
Pennsylvania.

Why were the elephants kicked out of
the swimming pool?
*Because they kept dropping their
trunks in the water.*

What did the witch call her baby
daughter?
Wanda.

What sort of fish would you find
in a shoe?
An eel.

Is it hard to bury an elephant?
Yes, it's a huge undertaking.

What's the difference between a post box and an elephant's bottom?
If you don't know, I'm certainly not going to ask you to post my letters.

How do you make a hippo sandwich?
Get a very large loaf, a few buckets of butter and tuck in!

Why is it easy to swindle a sheep?
Because you can just pull the wool over its eyes.

How can you tell a male dinosaur from a female dinosaur?
Ask a question and if he answers, it's male, but if she answers, it's female.

If King Kong went to Hong Kong, played ping pong, had a sing song and then died, what would they put on his coffin?
A lid.

Why can you never swindle a snake?
Because it's impossible to pull its leg.

Why was the butcher worried?
Because his job was at steak.

What's the difference between an elephant with a thorn in its foot and a storm cloud?
One roars with pain and the other pours with rain.

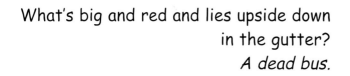

What's big and red and lies upside down
in the gutter?
A dead bus.

What's the best way to get King Kong
begging on his knees?
*Wave a four-ton banana in front of
his nose.*

Why do gorillas have big nostrils?
Because they have big fingers.

Why did the doll blush?
Because she saw the teddy bear.